M000248593

Baby Afghans

LEISURE ARTS, INC. • Maumelle, Arkansas

SOFT ZIGZAGS

Finished Size: 35" x 42"

(89 cm x 106.5 cm)

SHOPPING LIST

Yarn (Medium Weight)

[5 ounces, 256 yards

(142 grams, 234 meters) per skein]:

☐ White - 4 skeins

☐ Blue - 4 skeins

Crochet Hook

☐ Size I (5.5 mm)

or size needed for gauge

GAUGE INFORMATION

37 sts (point to point) = 7" (18 cm);

12 rows = 4" (10 cm)

Gauge Swatch: 7" wide x 4" high

(18 cm x 10 cm)

With White, ch 36.

Row 1: Sc in second ch from hook and in next 16 chs, 3 sc in next ch, sc in last 17 chs: 37 sc.

Rows 2-12: Ch 1, turn; skip first sc, sc in next 17 sc, 3 sc in next sc, sc in next 16 sc, skip next sc, sc in last sc. Finish off.

STITCH GUIDE

LONG DOUBLE CROCHET

(abbreviated Ldc)

YO, insert hook in st 2 rows **below** next sc *(Fig. 1)*, YO and pull up a loop even with last st made, (YO and draw through 2 loops on hook) twice.

Fig. 1

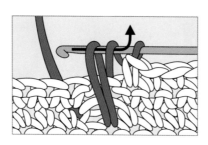

EXTENDED LONG DOUBLE

CROCHET *(abbreviated ex Ldc)*

YO, insert hook in st 3 rows **below** next sc, YO and pull up a loop even with last st made, (YO and draw through 2 loops on hook) twice.

CHANGING COLORS

Insert hook in last sc, YO and pull up a loop, drop yarn, with new yarn *(Fig. 2)*, YO and draw through both loops on hook. Work over both ends.

Fig. 2

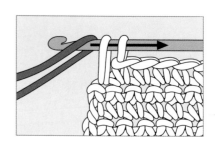

STRIPE SEQUENCE

★ 4 Rows of White, 4 rows of Blue *(Fig. 2)*; repeat from ★ 14 times **more**, work 2 rows of White.

INSTRUCTIONS

With White, ch 184.

Row 1: Sc in second ch from hook and in next 16 chs, 3 sc in next ch, sc in next 17 chs, ★ skip next 2 chs, sc in next 17 chs, 3 sc in next ch, sc in next 17 chs; repeat from ★ across: 185 sc.

Rows 2-4: Ch 1, turn; skip first sc, sc in next 17 sc, 3 sc in next sc, ★ sc in next 17 sc, skip next 2 sc, sc in next 17 sc, 3 sc in next sc; repeat from ★ 3 times **more**, sc in next 16 sc, skip next sc, sc in last sc.

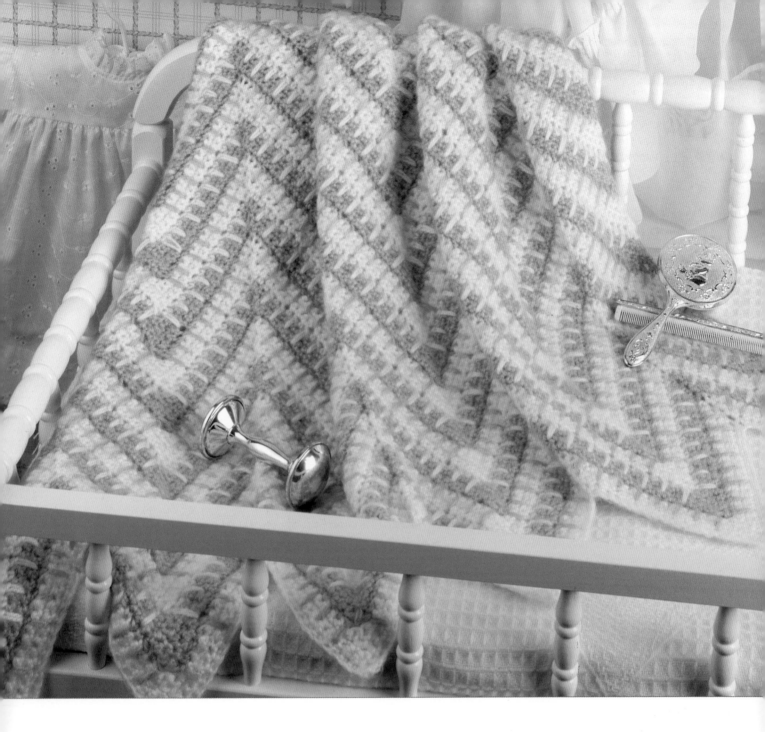

Row 5: Ch 1, turn; skip first sc, sc in next 2 sc, work Ldc, (sc in next sc, work ex Ldc, sc in next sc, work Ldc) 3 times, sc in next 2 sc, 3 sc in next sc, sc in next 2 sc, work Ldc, sc in next sc, (work ex Ldc, sc in next sc, work Ldc, sc in next sc) 3 times, ★ work ex Ldc, skip next 2 sc, work ex Ldc, sc in next sc, work Ldc, (sc in next sc, work ex Ldc, sc in next sc, work Ldc) 3 times, sc in next 2 sc, 3 sc in next sc, sc in next 2 sc, work Ldc, sc in next sc, (work ex Ldc, sc in next sc, work Ldc, sc in next sc) 3 times; repeat from ★ across to last 2 sc, skip next sc, sc in last sc.

Rows 6-8: Ch 1, turn; skip first sc, sc in next 17 sts, 3 sc in next sc, ★ sc in next 17 sts, skip next 2 sts, sc in next 17 sts, 3 sc in next sc; repeat from ★ 3 times **more**, sc in next 16 sts, skip next sc, sc in last sc.

Rows 9-122: Repeat Rows 5-8, 28 times; then repeat Rows 5 and 6 once **more**.

Finish off.

Design by Carole Prior.

 **EASY**

Finished Size: 37" x 49"
(94 cm x 124.5 cm)

SHOPPING LIST

Yarn (Light Weight)
[7 ounces, 575 yards
(198 grams, 525 meters) per skein]:
☐ 4 skeins

Crochet Hook
☐ Size F (3.75 mm)
or size needed for gauge

Additional Supplies
☐ Tapestry needle

GAUGE INFORMATION

Each Motif = 6" (15.25 cm)
Gauge Swatch: 2¼" (5.75 cm)
Work same as Motif for 3 rnds.

INSTRUCTIONS
Motif (Make 52)

Ch 4; join with slip st to form a ring.

Rnd 1 (Right side)**:** Ch 1, (sc in ring, ch 2) 6 times; join with slip st to first sc: 6 ch-2 sps.

Note: Loop a short piece of yarn around any stitch to mark Rnd 1 as **right** side.

Rnd 2: Slip st in first ch-2 sp, ch 1, sc in same sp and in next sc, ch 3, (sc in next ch-2 sp and in next sc, ch 3) 4 times, sc in last ch-2 sp and in same st as joining, ch 3; join with slip st to first sc: 12 sc and 6 ch-3 cps.

Markers are used to help distinguish the beginning of each round being worked. Place a 2" (5 cm) scrap piece of yarn around the first ch-3 of each round, moving the marker after each round is completed.

Rnd 3: Ch 3, skip next sc, 2 sc in next ch-3 sp, ★ sc in next sc, ch 3, 2 sc in next ch-3 sp; repeat from ★ 4 times **more**, sc in same st as joining; do **not** join, ▮▮ place marker: 18 sc.

Rnd 4: ★ Ch 3, 2 sc in next ch-3 sp, sc in next 2 sc; repeat from ★ around: 24 sc.

Rnd 5: ★ Ch 3, 2 sc in next ch-3 sp, sc in next 3 sc; repeat from ★ around: 30 sc.

Rnd 6: ★ Ch 3, 2 sc in next ch-3 sp, sc in next 4 sc; repeat from ★ around: 36 sc.

Rnd 7: ★ Ch 3, 2 sc in next ch-3 sp, sc in next 5 sc; repeat from ★ around: 42 sc.

Rnd 8: ★ Ch 3, 2 sc in next ch-3 sp, sc in next 6 sc; repeat from ★ around: 48 sc.

Rnd 9: ★ Ch 3, 2 sc in next ch-3 sp, sc in next 7 sc; repeat from ★ around: 54 sc.

Rnd 10: ★ Ch 3, 2 sc in next ch-3 sp, sc in next 8 sc; repeat from ★ around: 60 sc.

Rnd 11: ★ Ch 3, 2 sc in next ch-3 sp, sc in next 9 sc; repeat from ★ around: 66 sc.

Rnd 12: Ch 3, ★ 2 sc in next ch-3 sp, sc in next 10 sc, ch 3; repeat from ★ around, slip st in next sc; finish off: 72 sc.

Assembly

With **wrong** sides together, and working through **inside** loops, whipstitch Motifs together *(Fig. 9b, page 31)* forming 4 vertical strips of 7 Motifs each and 3 vertical strips of 8 Motifs each; then whipstitch strips together in same manner following Placement Diagram.

Edging

Rnd 1: With **right** side facing, join yarn with sc in any sc *(see Joining With Sc, page 30)*; sc in each sc around working 4 sc in each ch-3 sp and 2 sc in sp at each side of joining; join with slip st to first sc.

Rnd 2: Ch 1, do **not** turn; hdc in same st, ch 1, working from **left** to **right**, skip next sc, YO, insert hook in st to **right** of hook *(Fig. 3a)*, YO and draw through, under and to left of loop on hook (3 loops on hook) *(Fig. 3b)*, YO and draw through all 3 loops on hook *(Fig. 3c)*, **(reverse hdc made, Fig. 3d)**, ch 1, ★ work reverse hdc in next sc, ch 1, skip next sc; repeat from ★ around; join with slip st to first hdc, finish off.

Design by Carole Rutter Tippett.

Placement Diagram

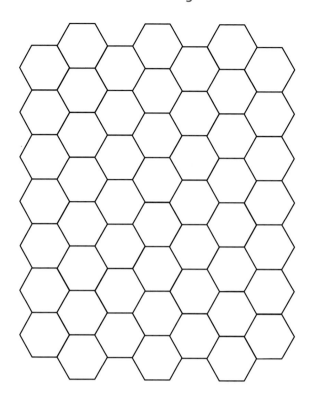

Fig. 3a

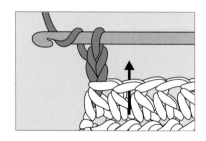

Fig. 3b

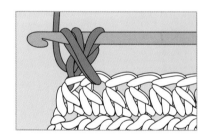

Fig. 3c

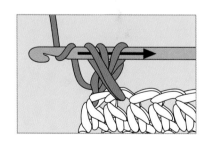

Fig. 3d

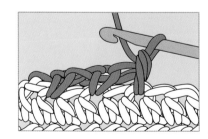

GRANNY'S LOVE

Shown on page 9.

 **INTERMEDIATE**

Finished Size: 37" x 42"
(94 cm x 106.5 cm)

SHOPPING LIST

Yarn (Light Weight) 🧶
[5 ounces, 358 yards
(141 grams, 328 meters) per skein]:
☐ White - 4 skeins
☐ Blue - one skein
☐ Yellow - one skein
☐ Pink - one skein
☐ Green - one skein

Crochet Hook
☐ Size F (3.75 mm)
  or size needed for gauge

Additional Supplies
☐ Tapestry needle

GAUGE INFORMATION
One Square = 2½" (6.25 cm)
  One Strip = 5" wide x 40" long
  (12.75 cm x 101.5 cm)
Gauge Swatch: 2½" (6.25 cm) square
  Work same as Square A.

INSTRUCTIONS
Strip A (Make 2)
SQUARE A (Make 15)
Rnd 1 (Right side): With Blue, ch 4, 2 dc in fourth ch from hook, ch 3, (3 dc in same st, ch 3) 3 times; join with slip st to top of beginning ch, finish off.

Note: Loop a short piece of yarn around any stitch to mark Rnd 1 as **right** side.

Rnd 2: With **right** side facing, join White with slip st in any ch-3 sp; ch 3 (**counts as first dc, now and throughout**), (2 dc, ch 3, 3 dc) in same sp, ch 1, ★ (3 dc, ch 3, 3 dc) in next ch-3 sp, ch 1; repeat from ★ around; join with slip st to first dc, finish off.

JOINING
With **wrong** sides together, working through **both** loops, and using White, whipstitch Squares together *(Fig. 9a, page 31)* forming 2 vertical Strips of 15 Squares each, beginning in center ch of one corner ch-3 and ending in center ch of next corner ch-3; do **not** join Strips.

EDGING
Rnd 1: With **right** side facing, 🎥 join White with sc in top right ch-3 sp

(see Joining With Sc, page 30); ch 3, sc in same sp, † ch 1, skip next dc, sc in next dc, ch 1, sc in next ch-1 sp, ch 1, skip next dc, sc in next dc, ch 1, (sc, ch 3, sc) in next ch-3 sp, ch 1, skip next dc, sc in next dc, ch 1, sc in next ch-1 sp, ch 1, skip next dc, sc in next dc, ch 1, ★ (sc in next sp, ch 1) twice, skip next dc, sc in next dc, ch 1, sc in next ch-1 sp, ch 1, skip next dc, sc in next dc, ch 1; repeat from ★ across to next ch-3 sp †, (sc, ch 3, sc) in ch-3 sp, repeat from † to † once; join with slip st to first sc: 160 sps.

Rnd 2: Slip st in first ch-3 sp, ch 1, (sc, ch 3, sc) in same sp, ch 1, (sc in next ch-1 sp, ch 1) across to next ch-3 sp, ★ (sc, ch 3, sc) in ch-3 sp, ch 1, (sc in next ch-1 sp, ch 1) across to next ch-3 sp; repeat from ★ around; join with slip st to first sc, finish off: 164 sps.

Rnd 3: With **right** side facing, join Yellow with slip st in top right ch-3 sp; ch 3, (2 dc, ch 3, 3 dc) in same sp, ch 1, skip next ch-1 sp, (3 dc in next ch-1 sp, ch 1, skip next ch-1 sp) across to next ch-3 sp, ★ (3 dc, ch 3, 3 dc) in ch-3 sp, ch 1, skip next ch-1 sp, (3 dc in next ch-1 sp, ch 1, skip next ch-1 sp) across to next ch-3 sp; repeat from ★ around; join with slip st to first dc, finish off.

Rnd 4: With **right** side facing, join White with slip st in any ch-3 sp; ch 3, (2 dc, ch 3, 3 dc) in same sp, ch 1, (3 dc in next ch-1 sp, ch 1) across to next ch-3 sp, ★ (3 dc, ch 3, 3 dc) in ch-3 sp, ch 1, (3 dc in next ch-1 sp, ch 1) across to next ch-3 sp; repeat from ★ around; join with slip st to first dc, finish off.

Strip B (Make 2)
SQUARE B (Make 15)
Work same as Square A working in the following color sequence: One rnd each of Pink and White.

JOINING
Work same as Strip A.

EDGING
Work same as Strip A working in the following color sequence: 2 Rnds White, one rnd each of Green and White.

Strip C (Make 2)
SQUARE C (Make 15)
Work same as Square A working in the following color sequence: One rnd each of Yellow and White.

JOINING
Work same as Strip A.

EDGING
Work same as Strip A working in the following color sequence: 2 Rnds White, one rnd **each** of Blue and White.

Strip D
SQUARE D (Make 15)
Work same as Square A working in the following color sequence: One rnd each of Green and White.

JOINING
Work same as Strip A.

EDGING
Work same as Strip A working in the following color sequence: 2 Rnds White, one rnd each of Pink and White.

Assembly
Whipstitch Strips together in the following order: A-B-C-D-A-B-C.

Border
Rnd 1: With **right** side facing, join White with sc in top right ch-3 sp; ch 3, sc in same sp, ch 1, † skip next dc, sc in next dc, ch 1, (sc in next ch-1 sp, ch 1, skip next dc, sc in next dc, ch 1) 4 times, ★ (sc in next sp, ch 1) twice, skip next dc, sc in next dc, ch 1, (sc in next ch-1 sp, ch 1, skip next dc, sc in next dc, ch 1) 4 times; repeat from ★ across to next ch-3 sp, (sc, ch 3, sc) in ch-3 sp, ch 1, skip next dc, sc in next dc, ch 1, (sc in next ch-1 sp, ch 1, skip next dc, sc in next dc, ch 1) across to next ch-3 sp †, (sc, ch 3, sc) in ch-3 sp, ch 1, repeat from † to † once; join with slip st to first sc.

Rnd 2: Slip st in first ch-3 sp, ch 1, (sc, ch 3, sc) in same sp, ch 1, (sc in next ch-1 sp, ch 1) across to next ch-3 sp, ★ (sc, ch 3, sc) in ch-3 sp, ch 1, (sc in next ch-1 sp, ch 1) across to next ch-3 sp; repeat from ★ around; join with slip st to first sc.

To work Corner Lace St, sc in sp indicated, ch 4, dc in fourth ch from hook, sc in same sp.

To work Lace St, ch 3, dc in third ch from hook.

Rnd 3: Slip st in first ch-3 sp, ch 1, work Corner Lace St in same sp, work Lace St, skip next ch-1 sp, (sc in next ch-1 sp, work Lace St, skip next ch-1 sp) across to next ch-3 sp, ★ work Corner Lace St in ch-3 sp, work Lace St, skip next ch-1 sp, (sc in next ch-1 sp, work Lace St, skip next ch-1 sp) across to next ch-3 sp; repeat from ★ around; join with slip st to first sc, finish off.

Design by Anne Halliday.

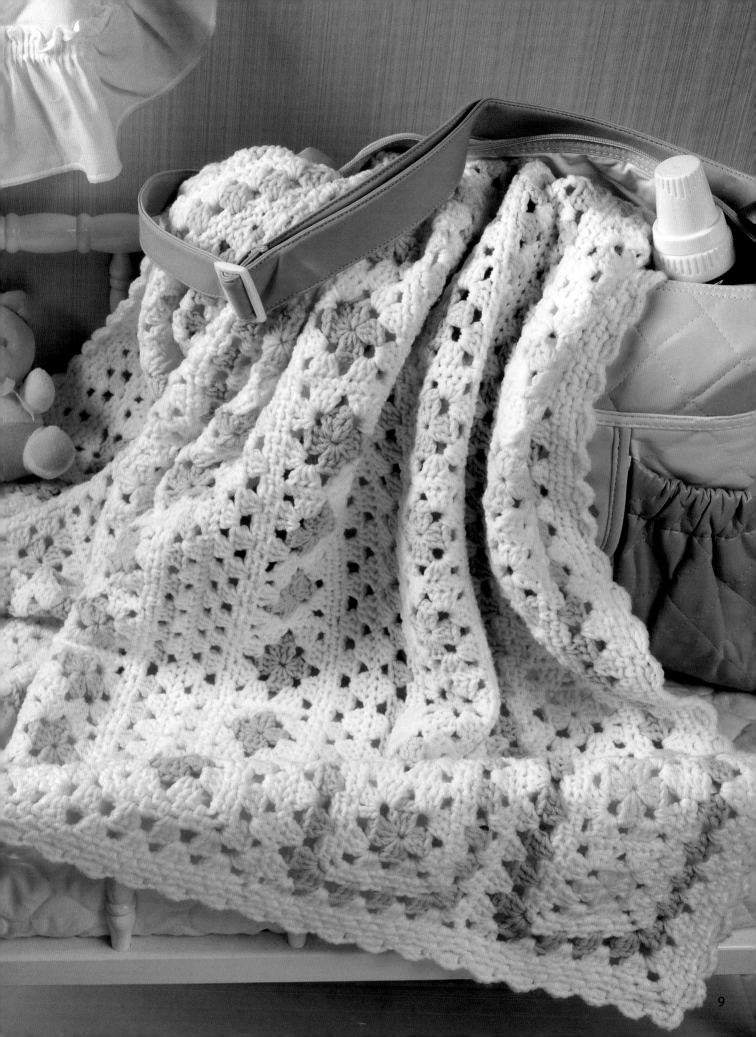

LITTLE BOY BLUE

 **INTERMEDIATE**

Blanket Finished Size:

35" x 48½" (89 cm x 123 cm)

SHOPPING LIST

Yarn (Light Weight)

**[3 ounces, 279 yards
(85 grams, 255 meters) per skein]:**

☐ Blanket - 7 skeins

☐ Booties - 75 yards
(68.5 meters)

Crochet Hook

As indicated below **or** size needed
for gauge:

Blanket

☐ Size F (3.75 mm)

Booties

☐ 0 to 3 months - size E (3.5 mm)

☐ 3 to 6 months - size F (3.75 mm)

Additional Supplies

☐ ¼" (7 mm) wide Ribbon -
32" (81.5 cm) length

☐ Yarn needle

GAUGE INFORMATION

BLANKET

In pattern,

16 dc and 8 rows = 4" (10 cm)

Gauge Swatch: 4¼" wide x 4" high
(10.75 cm x 10 cm)

Ch 19.

Work same as Blanket Body for 8 rows.
Finish off.

BOOTIES

0 to 3 months - 7 dc = 1½" (3.75 cm)

3 to 6 months - 6 dc = 1½" (3.75 cm)

Gauge Swatch:

0 to 3 months - 3¾" (9.5 cm)

3 to 6 months - 4" (10 cm)

Work same as Sole.

——— STITCH GUIDE ———

🎥 FRONT POST DOUBLE CROCHET
(abbreviated FPdc)

YO, insert hook from **front** to **back**
around post of st indicated
(Fig. 7, page 30), YO and pull up a
loop (3 loops on hook), (YO and draw
through 2 loops on hook) twice. Skip
st behind FPdc.

🎥 BACK POST DOUBLE CROCHET
(abbreviated BPdc)

YO, insert hook from **back** to **front**
around post of FPdc indicated
(Fig. 7, page 30), YO and pull up a
loop (3 loops on hook), (YO and draw
through 2 loops on hook) twice. Skip
st in front of BPdc.

🎥 FRONT POST CLUSTER
(abbreviated FP Cluster)

★ YO, insert hook from **front** to
back around post of st indicated
(Fig. 7, page 30), YO and pull up a
loop, YO and draw through 2 loops
on hook; repeat from ★ once **more**,
YO and draw through all 3 loops on
hook. Skip st behind FP Cluster.

INSTRUCTIONS
Blanket
BODY

Ch 127, place a marker in third ch from hook for st placement.

Row 1: Dc in fourth ch from hook **(3 skipped chs count as first dc)** and in each ch across: 125 dc.

Row 2 (Right side)**:** Ch 3 **(counts as first dc, now and throughout),** turn; dc in next 4 dc, ★ work FPdc around next dc, dc in next 2 dc, work FP Cluster around next dc, dc in next 2 dc, work FPdc around next dc, dc in next 5 dc; repeat from ★ across: 95 dc, 20 FPdc, and 10 FP Clusters.

Note: Loop a short piece of yarn around any stitch to mark Row 2 as **right** side.

Row 3: Ch 3, turn; dc in next 4 dc, (work BPdc around next FPdc, dc in next 5 sts) across: 105 dc and 20 BPdc.

Row 4: Ch 3, turn; dc in next dc, work FP Cluster around next dc, dc in next 2 dc, ★ work FPdc around next BPdc, dc in next 5 dc, work FPdc around next BPdc, dc in next 2 dc, work FP Cluster around next dc, dc in next 2 dc; repeat from ★ across: 94 dc, 20 FPdc, and 11 FP Clusters.

Row 5: Ch 3, turn; dc in next 4 sts, (work BPdc around next FPdc, dc in next 5 sts) across: 105 dc and 20 BPdc.

Row 6: Ch 3, turn; dc in next 4 dc, ★ work FPdc around next BPdc, dc in next 2 dc, work FP Cluster around next dc, dc in next 2 dc, work FPdc around next BPdc, dc in next 5 dc; repeat from ★ across: 95 dc, 20 FPdc, and 10 FP Clusters.

Repeat Rows 3-6 for pattern until Body measures approximately 44½" (113 cm) from beginning ch, ending by working a **wrong** side row; do **not** finish off.

EDGING

Rnd 1: Ch 3, turn; (2 dc, ch 1, 3 dc) in first dc, dc in each st across to last dc, (3 dc, ch 1, 3 dc) in last dc; work 177 dc evenly spaced across end of rows; working in  free loops of beginning ch *(Fig. 6, page 30)*, (3 dc, ch 1, 3 dc) in marked ch, dc in each ch across to last ch, (3 dc, ch 1, 3 dc) in last ch; work 177 dc evenly spaced across end of rows; join with slip st to first dc: 624 dc and 4 ch-1 sps.

Rnd 2: Ch 3, do **not** turn; skip next dc, work FP Cluster around next dc, ch 3, skip next corner ch-1 sp, work FP Cluster around next dc, ★ skip next dc, dc in next 5 dc, (work FP Cluster around next dc, dc in next 5 dc) across to within 2 dc of next corner ch-1 sp, skip next dc, work FP Cluster around next dc, ch 3, skip next corner ch-1 sp, work FP Cluster around next dc; repeat from ★ 2 times **more**, skip next dc, (dc in next 5 dc, work FP Cluster around next dc) across to last 4 dc, dc in last 4 dc; join with slip st to first dc: 510 dc, 106 FP Clusters, and 4 ch-3 sps.

Rnd 3: Slip st in next FP Cluster and in next corner ch-3 sp, ch 3, (2 dc, ch 1, 3 dc) in same sp, work FP Cluster around next FP Cluster, skip next dc, dc in next 3 dc, ★ † skip next dc, work (FP Cluster, ch 3, FP Cluster) around next FP Cluster, skip next dc, dc in next 3 dc †; repeat from † to † across to within 2 sts of next corner ch-3 sp, skip next dc, work FP Cluster around next FP Cluster, (3 dc, ch 1, 3 dc) in next corner ch-3 sp, work FP Cluster around next FP Cluster, skip next dc, dc in next 3 dc; repeat from ★ 2 times **more**, then repeat from † to † across to last 2 sts, skip next st, work FP Cluster around last FP Cluster; join with slip st to first dc: 330 dc, 204 FP Clusters, and 102 sps.

Rnd 4: Ch 1, **turn**; sc in same st as joining and in each st around, working 3 sc in each ch-3 sp and one sc in each ch-1 sp; join with slip st to first sc, finish off.

Booties
SOLE
Ch 13.

Rnd 1 (Right side)**:** 3 Sc in second ch from hook, sc in next 10 chs, 5 sc in last ch; working in free loops of beginning ch, sc in next 10 chs, 2 sc in next ch; join with slip st to 📹 Back Loop Only of first sc *(Fig. 5, page 30)*: 30 sc.

Note: Loop a short piece of yarn around any stitch to mark Rnd 1 as **right** side.

Rnd 2: Ch 3 **(counts as first dc, now and throughout unless otherwise indicated)**, working in Back Loops Only, 2 dc in next sc, hdc in next 3 sc, sc in next 4 sc, hdc in next 4 sc, 2 dc in each of next 2 sc, dc in next sc, 2 dc in each of next 2 sc, hdc in next 4 sc, sc in next 4 sc, hdc in next 3 sc, 2 dc in last sc; join with slip st to first dc, do **not** finish off: 36 sts.

SIDES
Rnd 1: Ch 3, dc in Back Loop Only of next st and each st around; join with slip st **both** loops of first dc.

Rnd 2: Ch 3, working in both loops, dc in next dc, work FP Cluster around next dc, dc in next 2 dc, work FPdc around next dc, ★ dc in next 2 dc, work FP Cluster around next dc, dc in next 2 dc, work FPdc around next dc; repeat from ★ around; join with slip st to first dc: 24 dc, 6 FPdc, and 6 FP Clusters.

📹 *To double crochet 2 together (abbreviated dc2tog) (uses next 2 sts),* ★ YO, insert hook in **next** st, YO and pull up a loop, YO and draw through 2 loops on hook; repeat from ★ once **more**, YO and draw through all 3 loops on hook **(counts as one dc)**.

Rnd 3: Ch 1, sc in same st as joining and in next 13 sts, dc2tog, (dc in next dc, dc2tog) 3 times, sc in last 11 sts; join with slip st to first sc: 32 sts.

Rnd 4: Ch 1, sc in same st as joining and in next 13 sc, dc2tog 4 times, sc in last 10 sc; join with slip st to first sc, do **not** finish off: 28 sts.

CUFF
Rnd 1 (Eyelet rnd)**:** Ch 3 **(counts as first hdc plus ch 1)**, skip next st, (hdc in next st, ch 1, skip next st) 5 times, (dc in next st, ch 1, skip next st) 5 times, (hdc in next st, ch 1, skip next st) 3 times; join with slip st to first hdc: 14 ch-1 sps.

Rnd 2: Ch 1, sc in same st as joining, 2 sc in each of next 7 ch-1 sps, sc in next dc, 2 sc in each of next 7 ch-1 sps; join with slip st to first sc: 30 sc.

Rnd 3: Ch 3, dc in next sc and in each sc around; join with slip st to first dc.

Rnd 4: Ch 3, dc in next 2 dc, skip next dc, work (FP Cluster, ch 3, FP Cluster) around next dc, skip next dc, ★ dc in next 3 dc, skip next dc, work (FP Cluster, ch 3, FP Cluster) around next dc, skip next dc; repeat from ★ around; join with slip st to first dc: 15 dc, 10 FP Clusters, and 5 ch-3 sps.

Rnd 5: Ch 1, **turn**; sc in next FP Cluster, 3 sc in next ch-3 sp, (sc in next 5 sts, 3 sc in next ch-3 sp) around to last 4 sts, sc in last 4 sts; join with slip st to first sc, finish off.

Beginning at center front, weave a 16" (40.5 cm) length of ribbon through Eyelet rnd.

Designs by Mary Ann Sipes.

BABY LOVE

 **EASY**

Finished Size: 34¼" x 45"
(87 cm x 114.5 cm)

SHOPPING LIST

Yarn (Light Weight) **[3]**
[1.75 ounces, 161 yards
(50 grams, 147 meters) per skein]:
☐ White - 8 skeins
☐ Pink - 6 skeins

Crochet Hook
☐ Size G (4 mm)
or size needed for gauge

GAUGE INFORMATION

In pattern,
13 sts and 12 rows = 3¼" (8.25 cm)
Gauge Swatch: 7" wide x 2½" high
(17.75 cm x 6.25 cm)
Ch 29.
Work same as Afghan for 9 rows.
Finish off.

Each row is worked across length
of Afghan. When joining yarn and
finishing off, leave a 7" (18 cm) end to
be worked into fringe.

STITCH GUIDE

📹 DOUBLE TREBLE CROCHET
(abbreviated dtr)

YO 3 times, insert hook in sc
indicated, YO and pull up a loop
(5 loops on hook), (YO and draw
through 2 loops on hook) 4 times.

INSTRUCTIONS

With Pink, ch 181.

Row 1 (Wrong side): Sc in second
ch from hook and in each ch across;
finish off: 180 sc.

Note: Loop a short piece of yarn
around the back of any stitch on
Row 1 to mark **right** side.

Row 2: With **right** side facing, 📹 join
White with sc in first sc *(see Joining
With Sc, page 30)*; sc in next 3 sc,
★ ch 1, skip next sc, sc in next 2 sc,
ch 1, skip next sc, sc in next 4 sc;
repeat from ★ across; finish off: 136 sc
and 44 ch-1 sps.

Row 3: With **wrong** side facing,
📹 join White with dc in first sc *(see
Joining With Dc, page 30)*; dc in next
sc and in each sc and each ch-1 sp
across; finish off: 180 dc.

Row 4: With **right** side facing, join
Pink with sc in first dc; sc in next 3 dc,
📹 working in **front** of previous
rows, dtr in second skipped sc 3 rows
below, skip dc **behind** dtr on previous
row, sc in next 2 dc, working in **front**
of last dtr made, dtr in first skipped
sc 3 rows **below**, skip dc **behind**
dtr on previous row, sc in next 4 dc,
★ skip next skipped sc 3 rows **below**,
working in **front** of previous rows, dtr
in next skipped sc, skip dc **behind**
dtr on previous row, sc in next 2 dc,
working in **front** of last dtr made, dtr
in skipped sc 3 rows **below**, skip dc
behind dtr on previous row, sc in next
4 dc; repeat from ★ across; finish off:
136 sc and 44 dtr.

Row 5: With **wrong** side facing, join
Pink with sc in first sc; sc in next sc
and in each st across; finish off: 180 sc.

Row 6: With **right** side facing, join
White with sc in first sc; sc in next
7 sc, ch 1, skip next sc, sc in next 2 sc,
ch 1, ★ skip next sc, sc in next 4 sc,
ch 1, skip next sc, sc in next 2 sc, ch 1;
repeat from ★ across to last 9 sc, skip
next sc, sc in last 8 sc; finish off: 138 sc
and 42 ch-1 sps.

Row 7: With **wrong** side facing, join White with dc in first sc; dc in next sc and in each sc and each ch-1 sp across; finish off: 180 dc.

Row 8: With **right** side facing, join Pink with sc in first dc; sc in next 7 dc, working in **front** of previous rows, dtr in second skipped sc 3 rows **below**, skip dc **behind** dtr on previous row, sc in next 2 dc, working in **front** of last dtr made, dtr in first skipped sc 3 rows **below**, ★ skip dc **behind** dtr on previous row, sc in next 4 dc, skip next skipped sc 3 rows **below**, working in **front** of previous rows, dtr in next skipped sc, skip dc **behind** dtr on previous row, sc in next 2 dc, working in **front** of last dtr made, dtr in skipped sc 3 rows **below**; repeat from ★ across to last 9 dc, skip dc **behind** dtr on previous row, sc in last 8 dc; finish off: 138 sc and 42 dtr.

Row 9: With **wrong** side facing, join Pink with sc in first sc; sc in next sc and in each st across; finish off: 180 sc.

Rows 10-125: Repeat Rows 2-9, 14 times; then repeat Rows 2-5 once **more**.

Trim
FIRST SIDE
With **right** side facing, join Pink with sc in first sc on Row 125; sc in next sc and in each sc across; finish off.

SECOND SIDE
With **right** side facing and working in ⬛ free loops of beginning ch *(Fig. 6, page 30)*, join Pink with sc in first ch; sc in next ch and each ch across; finish off.

Fringe
Cut a piece of cardboard 5" wide x 6" long (12.5 cm x 16.5 cm). Wind the yarn **loosely** and evenly lengthwise around the cardboard until the card is filled, then cut across one end; repeat as needed.

⬛ With **wrong** side of short edge facing, using one corresponding color strand, draw the folded end up through a row and pull the loose ends through the folded end *(Fig. 4a)*; draw the knot up tightly *(Fig. 4b)*. Repeat across each short edge. Lay Afghan flat on a hard surface and trim the ends.

Fig. 4a

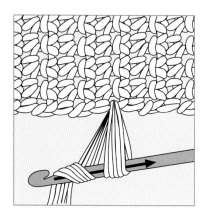

Fig. 4b

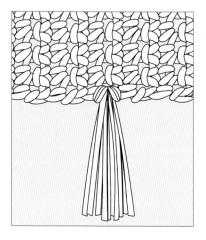

Design by Kay Meadors.

CONCENTRIC CIRCLES

Shown on page 19.

 EASY +

Finished Size: 38" wide x 50" high
(96.5 cm x 127 cm)

SHOPPING LIST

Yarn (Light Weight)
[5 ounces, 395 yards
(140 grams, 361 meters) per skein]:
- ☐ White - 2 skeins
- ☐ Blue - one skein
- ☐ Lilac - one skein
- ☐ Green - one skein
- ☐ Mint - one skein
- ☐ Pink - one skein
- ☐ Yellow - one skein

Crochet Hook
- ☐ Size G (4 mm)
  or size needed for gauge

Additional Supplies
- ☐ Yarn needle

GAUGE INFORMATION
Each Square = 6" (15 cm)
Gauge Swatch:
  2¹⁄₈" (5.4 cm) square
Work same as Square through Rnd 2:
32 dc.

INSTRUCTIONS
Blue Square (Make 8)
With Blue, ch 4; join with slip st to form a ring.

Rnd 1 (Right side)**:** Ch 3 **(counts as first dc, now and throughout)**, 15 dc in ring; join with slip st to first dc, finish off: 16 dc.

Note: Loop a short piece of yarn around any stitch to mark Rnd 1 as **right** side.

Rnd 2: With **right** side facing, 🎥 join White with dc in any dc *(see Joining With Dc, page 30)*; dc in same st, 2 dc in next dc and in each dc around; join with slip st to first dc, finish off: 32 dc.

Rnd 3: With **right side** facing, join Blue with dc in any dc; dc in same st and in next dc, (2 dc in next dc, dc in next dc) around; join with slip st to first dc, finish off: 48 dc.

Rnd 4: With **right** side facing, join White with dc in any dc; dc in same st and in next 2 dc, (2 dc in next dc, dc in next 2 dc) around; join with slip st to first dc, finish off: 64 dc.

Rnd 5: With **right** side facing, 🎥 join Blue with sc in any dc *(see Joining With Sc, page 30)*; (ch 5, skip next 3 dc, sc in next dc) around to last 3 dc, ch 2, skip last 3 dc, dc in first sc to form last ch-5 sp: 16 sc and 16 ch-5 sps.

Rnd 6: Ch 1, 3 sc in last sp made, 5 sc in next ch-5 sp and in each ch-5 sp around, 2 sc in same sp as first sc; join with slip st to first sc: 80 sc.

🎥 *To work treble crochet (abbreviated tr), YO twice, insert hook in sc indicated, YO and pull up a loop (4 loops on hook), (YO and draw through 2 loops on hook) 3 times.*

Rnd 7: Ch 4 **(counts as first tr)**, ★ † tr in next 2 sc, dc in next 2 sc, hdc in next 2 sc, sc in next 7 sc, hdc in next 2 sc, dc in next 2 sc, tr in next 2 sc †, (tr, ch 3, tr) in next sc; repeat from ★ 2 times **more**, then repeat from † to † once, tr in same st as first tr, 🎥 ch 1, hdc in first tr to form last corner ch-3 sp: 84 sts and 4 ch-3 sps.

Rnd 8: Ch 3, dc in last corner sp made and in next 21 sts, ★ (2 dc, ch 2, 2 dc) in next corner ch-3 sp, dc in next 21 sts; repeat from ★ 2 times **more**, 2 dc in same sp as first dc, ch 1, sc in first dc to form last corner ch-2 sp; finish off leaving a long end for sewing: 100 dc and 4 ch-2 sps.

Remaining Squares
(Make 40)
Replacing Blue with new color, make 8 each using the following colors: Green, Lilac, Mint, Pink, Yellow.

Assembly
With **wrong** sides together, working through **inside** loops, and using long end, whipstitch Squares together in random order *(Fig. 9b, page 31)*, forming 6 vertical strips of 8 Squares each, beginning in second st of corner ch-2 and ending in first st of next corner ch-2; then whipstitch Strips together in same manner.

Edging
With **right** side facing, join White with dc in any st; dc evenly around working 3 dc in each dc corner; join with slip st to first dc, finish off.

Design by Melissa Leapman.

PRECIOUS IN PINK

Blanket Finished Size: 35" x 45½" (89 cm x 115.5 cm)

SHOPPING LIST

Yarn (Light Weight)
[5 ounces, 362 yards (140 grams, 331 meters) per skein]:
☐ Blanket - 4 skeins
☐ Booties - 65 yards (59 meters)

Crochet Hook
As indicated below **or** size needed for gauge:

Blanket
☐ Size F (3.75 mm)

Booties
☐ 0 to 3 months - size E (3.5 mm)
☐ 3 to 6 months - size F (3.75 mm)

Additional Supplies
☐ ¼" (7 mm) wide Ribbon - 32" (81.5 cm) length
☐ Yarn needle

GAUGE INFORMATION

BLANKET
In pattern,
16 sts and 8 rows = 4" (10 cm)
One Panel = 10¼" (26 cm) wide
Gauge Swatch: 4" (10 cm) square
Ch 18.
Row 1: Dc in fourth ch from hook **(3 skipped chs count as first dc)** and in each ch across: 16 dc.
Rows 2-8: Ch 3 **(counts as first dc)**, turn; dc in next dc and in each dc across.
Finish off.

BOOTIES
0 to 3 months - 7 dc = 1¼" (3.75 cm)
3 to 6 months - 6 dc = 1½" (3.75 cm)
Gauge Swatch:
0 to 3 months - 3¾" (9.5 cm)
3 to 6 months - 4" (10 cm)
Work same as Sole.

INSTRUCTIONS
Blanket
PANEL (Make 3)
Ch 43, place a marker in third ch from hook for st placement.

Row 1 (Right side): Dc in fourth ch from hook **(3 skipped chs count as first dc)** and in next 2 chs, ch 1, ★ skip next ch, dc in next 3 chs, ch 1; repeat from ★ across to last 5 chs, skip next ch, dc in last 4 chs: 32 dc and 9 ch-1 sps.

Note: Loop a short piece of yarn around any stitch to mark Row 1 as **right** side and bottom edge.

Row 2: Ch 3 **(counts as first dc, now and throughout)**, turn; dc in next dc, ch 1, ★ skip next dc, dc in next dc and in next ch-1 sp, dc in next dc, ch 1; repeat from ★ across to last 3 dc, skip next dc, dc in last 2 dc: 31 dc and 10 ch-1 sps.

Row 3: Ch 3, turn; dc in next dc and in next ch-1 sp, ★ dc in next dc, ch 1, skip next dc, dc in next dc and in next ch-1 sp; repeat from ★ across to last 2 dc, dc in last 2 dc: 32 dc and 9 ch-1 sps.

Row 4: Ch 3, turn; dc in next dc, ch 1, ★ skip next dc, (dc in next dc, ch 1) twice; repeat from ★ across to last 3 dc, skip next dc, dc in last 2 dc: 22 dc and 19 ch-1 sps.

Row 5: Ch 3, turn; dc in next dc and in next ch-1 sp, dc in next dc, (ch 1, dc in next dc) across to last ch-1 sp, dc in last ch-1 sp and in last 2 dc: 24 dc and 17 ch-1 sps.

Row 6: Ch 3, turn; dc in next dc, ch 1, skip next dc, (dc in next dc, ch 1) across to last 3 dc, skip next dc, dc in last 2 dc: 22 dc and 19 ch-1 sps.

Row 7: Ch 3, turn; dc in next dc and in next ch-1 sp, ★ (dc in next dc, ch 1) 8 times, dc in next dc and in next ch-1 sp; repeat from ★ once **more**, dc in last 2 dc: 25 dc and 16 ch-1 sps.

Row 8: Ch 3, turn; dc in next dc, ch 1, skip next dc, (dc in next dc, ch 1) 7 times, dc in next dc and in next ch-1 sp, dc in next 3 dc and in next ch-1 sp, (dc in next dc, ch 1) 8 times, skip next dc, dc in last 2 dc.

Row 9: Ch 3, turn; dc in next dc and in next ch-1 sp, (dc in next dc, ch 1) 6 times, dc in next dc and in next ch-1 sp, dc in next 3 dc, ch 1, skip next dc, dc in next 3 dc and in next ch-1 sp, (dc in next dc, ch 1) 6 times, dc in next dc and in next ch-1 sp, dc in last 2 dc: 28 dc and 13 ch-1 sps.

Row 10: Ch 3, turn; dc in next dc, ch 1, skip next dc, (dc in next dc, ch 1) 5 times, dc in next dc and in next ch-1 sp, dc in next 3 dc, ch 1, skip next dc, (dc in next dc, ch 1) twice, skip next dc, dc in next 3 dc and in next ch-1 sp, (dc in next dc, ch 1) 6 times, skip next dc, dc in last 2 dc: 26 dc and 15 ch-1 sps.

Row 11: Ch 3, turn; dc in next dc and in next ch-1 sp, (dc in next dc, ch 1) 4 times, dc in next dc and in next ch-1 sp, dc in next 3 dc, ch 1, skip next dc, (dc in next dc, ch 1) 4 times, skip next dc, dc in next 3 dc and in next ch-1 sp, (dc in next dc, ch 1) 4 times, dc in next dc and in next ch-1 sp, dc in last 2 dc: 28 dc and 13 ch-1 sps.

Row 12: Ch 3, turn; dc in next dc, ch 1, skip next dc, (dc in next dc, ch 1) 3 times, dc in next dc and in next ch-1 sp, dc in next 3 dc, ch 1, skip next dc, (dc in next dc, ch 1) 6 times, skip next dc, dc in next 3 dc and in next ch-1 sp, (dc in next dc, ch 1) 4 times, skip next dc, dc in last 2 dc: 26 dc and 15 ch-1 sps.

Row 13: Ch 3, turn; dc in next dc and in next ch-1 sp, (dc in next dc, ch 1) twice, dc in next dc and in next ch-1 sp, dc in next 3 dc, ch 1, skip next dc, (dc in next dc, ch 1) 3 times, dc in next dc and in next ch-1 sp, (dc in next dc, ch 1) 4 times, skip next dc, dc in next 3 dc and in next ch-1 sp, (dc in next dc, ch 1) twice, dc in next dc and in next ch-1 sp, dc in last 2 dc: 29 dc and 12 ch-1 sps.

Row 14: Ch 3, turn; dc in next dc, ch 1, skip next dc, (dc in next dc, ch 1) twice, dc in next 5 dc, ch 1, (dc in next dc, ch 1) 3 times, dc in next 3 dc, ch 1, (dc in next dc, ch 1) 3 times, dc in next 5 dc, ch 1, (dc in next dc, ch 1) twice, skip next dc, dc in last 2 dc: 27 dc and 14 ch-1 sps.

Row 15: Ch 3, turn; dc in next dc and in next ch-1 sp, (dc in next dc, ch 1) twice, dc in next 5 dc, ch 1, (dc in next dc, ch 1) twice, dc in next dc and in next ch-1 sp, dc in next 3 dc and in next ch-1 sp, (dc in next dc, ch 1) 3 times, dc in next 5 dc, ch 1, dc in next dc, ch 1, dc in next dc and in next ch-1 sp, dc in last 2 dc: 31 dc and 10 ch-1 sps.

Row 16: Ch 3, turn; dc in next dc, ch 1, skip next dc, (dc in next dc, ch 1) 3 times, skip next dc, ★ dc in next 3 dc and in next ch-1 sp, (dc in next dc and in next ch-1 sp) twice, dc in next 3 dc, ch 1, skip next dc; repeat from ★ once **more**, (dc in next dc, ch 1) 3 times, skip next dc, dc in last 2 dc: 32 dc and 9 ch-1 sps.

Row 17: Ch 3, turn; dc in next dc and in next ch-1 sp, (dc in next dc, ch 1) 4 times, skip next dc, dc in next 7 dc, ch 1, skip next dc, (dc in next dc, ch 1) twice, skip next dc, dc in next 7 dc, ch 1, skip next dc, (dc in next dc, ch 1) 3 times, dc in next dc and in next ch-1 sp, dc in last 2 dc: 30 dc and 11 ch-1 sps.

Row 18: Ch 3, turn; dc in next dc, ch 1, skip next dc, (dc in next dc, ch 1) 5 times, skip next dc, (dc in next dc, ch 1, skip next dc) twice, (dc in next dc, ch 1) 4 times, skip next dc, (dc in next dc, ch 1, skip next dc) twice, (dc in next dc, ch 1) 5 times, skip next dc, dc in last 2 dc: 22 dc and 19 ch-1 sps.

Row 19: Ch 3, turn; dc in next dc and in next ch-1 sp, dc in next dc, (ch 1, dc in next dc) across to last ch-1 sp, dc in last ch-1 sp and in last 2 dc: 24 dc and 17 ch-1 sps.

Row 20: Ch 3, turn; dc in next dc, ch 1, skip next dc, (dc in next dc, ch 1) across to last 3 dc, skip next dc, dc in last 2 dc: 22 dc and 19 ch-1 sps.

Row 21: Ch 3, turn; dc in next dc and in next ch-1 sp, ★ dc in next dc, ch 1, dc in next dc and in next ch-1 sp; repeat from ★ across to last 2 dc, dc in last 2 dc: 32 dc and 9 ch-1 sps.

Rows 22-83: Repeat Rows 2-21, 3 times; then repeat Rows 2 and 3 once **more**; do **not** finish off.

Border

With **right** side facing and working in end of rows, (slip st, ch 3, dc) in Row 83, 2 dc in next row and in each row across; working in  free loops of beginning ch *(Fig. 6, page 30)*, (2 dc, ch 2, 2 dc) in first ch, dc in each ch across to marked ch, (2 dc, ch 2, 2 dc) in marked ch; working in end of rows, 2 dc in each row across; (2 dc, ch 2, 2 dc) in first dc on Row 83, dc in each dc and in each ch across to last dc, (2 dc, ch 2, 2 dc) in last dc; join with slip st to first dc, finish off: 426 dc and 4 ch-2 sps.

Assembly

Join Panels as follows:
Place two Panels with **wrong** sides of long edges together with bottom edges at the same end. Beginning in second ch of first corner and working through **inside** loops of each stitch of both pieces, whipstitch Panels together *(Fig. 9b, page 31)*, ending in first ch of next corner.

Edging

Rnd 1: With **right** side of short edge facing, join yarn with slip st in first corner ch-2 sp; ch 5 (**counts as first dc plus ch 2**), 2 dc in same corner sp, † ch 1, (skip next dc, dc in next 3 dc, ch 1) 10 times, skip next dc, dc in next 2 dc and in next ch, ch 1, skip next joining and next ch, dc in next 3 dc, ch 1, (skip next dc, dc in next 3 dc, ch 1) 10 times, skip next ch and next joining, dc in next ch and in next 2 dc, ch 1, skip next dc, (dc in next 3 dc, ch 1, skip next dc) 10 times, (2 dc, ch 2, 2 dc) in next corner ch-2 sp †, (ch 1, skip next dc, dc in next 3 dc) across to within 2 dc of next corner ch-2 sp, ch 1, skip next 2 dc, (2 dc, ch 2, 2 dc) in corner ch-2 sp, repeat from † to † once, ch 1, skip next 2 dc, (dc in next 3 dc, ch 1, skip next dc) across, dc in same corner sp as joining; join with slip st to first dc: 466 dc and 4 ch-2 sps.

Rnds 2 and 3: (Slip st, ch 5, 2 dc) in next corner sp, ★ † ch 1, skip next dc, (dc in next dc and in next ch-1 sp, dc in next dc, ch 1, skip next dc) across to next corner ch-2 sp †, (2 dc, ch 2, 2 dc) in corner sp; repeat from ★ 2 times **more**, then repeat from † to † once, dc in same corner sp as first dc; join with slip st to first dc.

Finish off.

Booties
SOLE
Ch 13.

Rnd 1 (Right side)**:** 3 Sc in second ch from hook, sc in next 10 chs, 5 sc in last ch; working in free loops of beginning ch, sc in next 10 chs, 2 sc in next ch; join with slip st to  Back Loop Only of first sc (*Fig. 5, page 30*): 30 sc.

Note: Loop a short piece of yarn around any stitch to mark Rnd 1 as **right** side.

Rnd 2: Ch 3 (**counts as first dc, now and throughout unless otherwise indicated**), working in Back Loops Only, 2 dc in next sc, dc in next 3 sc, hdc in next 4 sc, dc in next 4 sc, 2 dc in each of next 2 sc, dc in next sc, 2 dc in each of next 2 sc, dc in next 4 sc, hdc in next 4 sc, dc in next 3 sc, 2 dc in last sc; join with slip st to first dc, do **not** finish off: 36 sts.

SIDES
Rnd 1: Ch 3, dc in Back Loop Only of next st and each st around; join with slip st to first dc.

Rnd 2: Ch 3, dc in both loops of next dc and each dc around; join with slip st to first dc.

To double crochet 2 together (abbreviated dc2tog) (uses next 2 sts), ★ *YO, insert hook in* **next** *st, YO and pull up a loop, YO and draw through 2 loops on hook; repeat from ★ once* **more**, *YO and draw through all 3 loops on hook* (**counts as one dc**).

Rnd 3: Ch 1, sc in same st as joining and in next 11 dc, dc2tog, (dc in next dc, dc2tog) 3 times, sc in last 13 dc; join with slip st to first sc: 32 sts.

Rnd 4: Ch 1, sc in same st as joining and in next 11 sc, dc2tog 4 times, sc in last 12 sc; join with slip st to first sc: 28 sts.

CUFF
Rnd 1 (Eyelet rnd)**:** Ch 3 (**counts as first hdc plus ch 1**), skip next st, (hdc in next st, ch 1, skip next st) 4 times, (dc in next st, ch 1, skip next st) 5 times, (hdc in next st, ch 1, skip next st) 4 times; join with slip st to first hdc: 14 ch-1 sps.

Rnd 2: Ch 1, 2 sc in each ch-1 sp around; join with slip st to first sc: 28 sc.

Rnd 3: Ch 4 (**counts as first dc plus ch 1, now and throughout**), ★ skip next sc, dc in next 3 sc, ch 1; repeat from ★ around to last 3 sc, skip next sc, dc in last 2 sc; join with slip st to first dc: 21 dc and 7 ch-1 sps.

Rnd 4: Ch 3, dc in next ch-1 sp and in next dc, ch 1, skip next dc, ★ dc in next dc and in next ch-1 sp, dc in next dc, ch 1, skip next dc; repeat from ★ around; join with slip st to first dc.

Rnd 5: Ch 4, skip next dc, dc in next dc and in next ch-1 sp, ★ dc in next dc, ch 1, skip next dc, dc in next dc and in next ch-1 sp; repeat from ★ around; join with slip st to first dc, finish off.

Beginning at center front, weave a 16" (40.5 cm) length of ribbon through Eyelet rnd.

Designs by Mary Ann Sipes.

RIPPLES OF JOY

Shown on page 27.

■■□□ **EASY**

Finished Size: 36" (91.5 cm) diameter

SHOPPING LIST

Yarn (Medium Weight) 🧶**4**
[3.5 ounces, 200 yards
(100 grams, 182 meters) per
skein]:
☐ Dk Pink - 2 skeins
☐ White - 1 skein
☐ Pink - 2 skeins

Crochet Hook
☐ Size H (5 mm)
or size needed for gauge

GAUGE INFORMATION
Gauge Swatch: 4" (10 cm) diameter
Work same as Afghan through
Rnd 3.

INSTRUCTIONS
With Dk Pink, ch 6; join with slip st to
form a ring.

Rnd 1 (Right side)**:** Ch 5 (**counts as
first dc plus ch 2**), (dc in ring, ch 2) 8
times; join with slip st to first dc: 9 dc
and 9 ch-2 sps.

Note: Loop a short piece of yarn
around any stitch to mark Rnd 1 as
right side.

Rnd 2: Ch 1, 5 sc in each ch-2 sp
around; join with slip st to first sc:
45 sc.

Rnd 3: Slip st in next sc, ch 3 (**counts
as first dc, now and throughout**),
3 dc in next sc, dc in next sc, skip next
2 sc, ★ dc in next sc, 3 dc in next sc, dc
in next sc, skip next 2 sts; repeat from
★ around; join with slip st to first dc.

Rnd 4: Ch 1, **turn**; sc in next 2 dc, 3 sc
in next dc, (sc in next 4 dc, 3 sc in next
dc) around to last 2 dc, sc in last 2 dc;
join with slip st to first sc: 63 sc.

Rnd 5: Slip st in next sc and in
📹 Front Loop Only of next sc *(Fig. 5,
page 30)*, ch 3, turn; working in
📹 Back Loops Only, dc in next sc, skip
next 2 sc, dc in next 2 sc, 3 dc in next
sc, ★ dc in next 2 sc, skip next 2 sc,
dc in next 2 sc, 3 dc in next sc; repeat
from ★ around; join with slip st to
first dc.

Rnd 6: Ch 1, turn; working in both
loops, sc in same st as joining and in
next dc, 3 sc in next dc, (sc in next
6 dc, 3 sc in next dc) around to last
4 dc, sc in last 4 dc; join with slip st to
Front Loop Only of first sc: 81 sc.

Rnd 7: Ch 3, turn; working in Back
Loops Only, skip next 2 sc, dc in next
3 sc, 3 dc in next sc, ★ dc in next 3 sc,
skip next 2 sc, dc in next 3 sc, 3 dc in
next sc; repeat from ★ around to last
2 sc, dc in last 2 sc; join with slip st to
first dc.

Rnd 8: Ch 1, turn; working in both
loops, sc in next 3 dc, 3 dc in next
dc, (sc in next 8 dc, 3 sc in next dc)
around to last 5 dc, sc in last 5 dc; join
with slip st to first sc, finish off: 99 sc.

Rnd 9: With **right** side facing and
working in Back Loops Only, 📹 join
White with dc in same sc as joining
(see Joining With Dc, page 30); skip
next 2 sc, dc in next 4 sc, (dc, ch 2, dc)
in next sc, ★ dc in next 4 sc, skip next
2 sc, dc in next 4 sc, (dc, ch 2, dc) in
next sc; repeat from ★ around to last
3 sc, dc in last 3 sc; join with slip st to
first dc: 90 dc and 9 ch-2 sps.

Rnd 10: Ch 1, turn; working in both loops, sc in same st as joining and in next 4 dc, 3 sc in next ch-2 sp, (sc in next 10 dc, 3 sc in next ch-2 sp) around to last 5 dc, sc in last 5 dc; join with slip st to first sc: 117 sc.

Rnd 11: Slip st in Front Loop Only of next sc, ch 3, turn; working in Back Loops Only, skip next 2 sts, dc in next 5 sc, (dc, ch 2, dc) in next sc, ★ dc in next 5 sc, skip next 2 sc, dc in next 5 sc, (dc, ch 2, dc) in next sc; repeat from ★ around to last 4 sc, dc in last 4 sc; join with slip st to first sc: 108 dc and 9 ch-2 sps.

Rnd 12: Ch 1, turn; working in both loops, sc in same st as joining and in next 5 dc, 3 sc in next ch-2 sp, (sc in next 12 dc, 3 sc in next ch-2 sp) around to last 6 dc, sc in last 6 dc; join with slip st to first sc: 135 sc.

Rnd 13: Slip st in Front Loop Only of next sc, ch 3, turn; working in Back Loops Only, skip next 2 sts, dc in next 6 sc, (dc, ch 2, dc) in next sc, ★ dc in next 6 sc, skip next 2 sc, dc in next 6 sc, (dc, ch 2, dc) in next sc; repeat from ★ around to last 5 sc, dc in last 5 sc; join with slip st to first dc: 126 dc and 9 ch-2 sps.

Rnd 14: Ch 1, turn; working in both loops, sc in same st as joining and in next 6 dc, 3 sc in next ch-2 sp, (sc in next 14 dc, 3 sc in next ch-2 sp) around to last 7 dc, sc in last 7 dc; join with slip st to first sc, finish off: 153 sc.

Rnd 15: With **right** side facing and working in Back Loops Only, join Dk Pink with dc in sc **before** joining sc; skip next 2 sc, dc in next 7 sc, (dc, ch 2, dc) in next sc, ★ dc in next 7 sc, skip next 2 sc, dc in next 7 sc, (dc, ch 2, dc) in next sc; repeat from ★ around to last 6 sc, dc in last 6 sc; join with slip st to first dc: 144 dc and 9 ch-2 sps.

Rnd 16: Ch 1, turn; working in both loops, sc in same st as joining and in next 7 dc, 3 sc in next ch-2 sp, (sc in next 16 dc, 3 sc in next ch-2 sp) around to last 8 dc, sc in last 8 dc; join with slip st to first sc: 171 sc.

Rnd 17: Slip st in Front Loop Only of next sc, ch 3, turn; working in Back Loops Only, skip next 2 sts, dc in next 8 sc, (dc, ch 2, dc) in next sc, ★ dc in next 8 sc, skip next 2 sc, dc in next 8 sc, (dc, ch 2, dc) in next sc; repeat from ★ around to last 7 sc, dc in last 7 sc; join with slip st to first dc: 162 dc and 9 ch-2 sps.

Rnd 18: Ch 1, turn; working in both loops, sc in same st as joining and in next 8 dc, 3 sc in next ch-2 sp, (sc in next 18 dc, 3 sc in next ch-2 sp) around to last 9 dc, sc in last 9 dc; join with slip st to first sc, finish off: 189 sc.

Rnd 19: With **right** side facing and working in Back Loops Only, join Pink with dc in sc **before** joining sc; skip next 2 sc, dc in next 9 sc, (dc, ch 2, dc) in next sc, ★ dc in next 9 sc, skip next 2 sc, dc in next 9 sc, (dc, ch 2, dc) in next sc; repeat from ★ around to last 8 sc, dc in last 8 sc; join with slip st to first dc: 180 dc and 9 ch-2 sps.

Rnd 20: Ch 1, turn; working in both loops, sc in same st as joining and in next 9 dc, 3 sc in next ch-2 sp, (sc in next 20 dc, 3 sc in next ch-2 sp) around to last 10 dc, sc in last 10 dc; join with slip st to first sc: 207 sc.

Rnd 21: Slip st in Front Loop Only of next sc, ch 3, turn; working in Back Loops Only, skip next 2 sts, dc in next 10 sc, (dc, ch 2, dc) in next sc, ★ dc in next 10 sc, skip next 2 sc, dc in next 10 sc, (dc, ch 2, dc) in next sc; repeat from ★ around to last 9 sc, dc in last 9 sc; join with slip st to first dc: 198 dc and 9 ch-2 sps.

Rnd 22: Ch 1, turn; working in both loops, sc in same st as joining and in next 10 dc, 3 sc in next ch-2 sp, (sc in next 22 dc, 3 sc in next ch-2 sp) around to last 11 dc, sc in last 11 dc; join with slip st to first sc: 225 sc.

Rnd 23: Slip st in Front Loop Only of next sc, ch 3, turn; working in Back Loops Only, skip next 2 sts, dc in next 11 sc, (dc, ch 2, dc) in next sc, ★ dc in next 11 sc, skip next 2 sc, dc in next 11 sc, (dc, ch 2, dc) in next sc; repeat from ★ around to last 10 sc, dc in last 10 sc; join with slip st to first dc: 216 dc and 9 ch-2 sps.

Rnd 24: Ch 1, turn; working in both loops, sc in same st as joining and in next 11 dc, 3 sc in next ch-2 sp, (sc in next 24 dc, 3 sc in next ch-2 sp) around to last 12 dc, sc in last 12 dc; join with slip st to first sc, finish off: 243 sc.

Rnd 25: With **right** side facing and working in Back Loops Only, join White with dc in sc **before** joining sc; skip next 2 sc, dc in next 12 sc, (dc, ch 2, dc) in next sc, ★ dc in next 12 sc, skip next 2 sc, dc in next 12 sc, (dc, ch 2, dc) in next sc; repeat from ★ around to last 11 sc, dc in last 11 sc; join with slip st to first dc: 234 dc and 9 ch-2 sps.

Rnd 26: Ch 1, turn; working in both loops, sc in same st as joining and in next 12 dc, 3 sc in next ch-2 sp, (sc in next 26 dc, 3 sc in next ch-2 sp) around to last 13 dc, sc in last 13 dc; join with slip st to first sc, finish off: 261 sc.

Rnd 27: With **right** side facing and working in Back Loops Only, join Dk Pink with dc in sc **before** joining sc; skip next 2 sc, dc in next 13 sc, (dc, ch 2, dc) in next sc, ★ dc in next 13 sc, skip next 2 sc, dc in next 13 sc, (dc, ch 2, dc) in next sc; repeat from ★ around to last 12 sc, dc in last 12 sc; join with slip st to first dc: 252 dc and 9 ch-2 sps.

Rnd 28: Ch 1, turn; working in both loops, sc in same st as joining and in next 13 dc, 3 sc in next ch-2 sp, (sc in next 28 dc, 3 sc in next ch-2 sp) around to last 14 dc, sc in last 14 dc; join with slip st to first sc: 279 sc.

Rnd 29: Slip st in Front Loop Only of next sc, ch 3, turn; working in Back Loops Only, skip next 2 sts, dc in next 14 sc, (dc, ch 2, dc) in next sc, ★ dc in next 14 sc, skip next 2 sc, dc in next 14 sc, (dc, ch 2, dc) in next sc; repeat from ★ around to last 13 sc, dc in last 13 sc; join with slip st to first dc: 270 dc and 9 ch-2 sps.

Rnd 30: Ch 1, turn; working in both loops, sc in same st as joining and in next 14 dc, 3 sc in next ch-2 sp, (sc in next 30 dc, 3 sc in next ch-2 sp) around to last 15 dc, sc in last 15 dc; join with slip st to first sc: 297 sc.

Rnd 31: Slip st in Front Loop Only of next sc, ch 3, turn; working in Back Loops Only, skip next 2 sts, dc in next 15 sc, (dc, ch 2, dc) in next sc, ★ dc in next 15 sc, skip next 2 sc, dc in next 15 sc, (dc, ch 2, dc) in next sc; repeat from ★ around to last 14 sc, dc in last 14 sc; join with slip st to first dc: 288 dc and 9 ch-2 sps.

Rnd 32: Ch 1, turn; working in both loops, sc in same st as joining and in next 15 dc, 3 sc in next ch-2 sp, (sc in next 32 dc, 3 sc in next ch-2 sp) around to last 16 dc, sc in last 16 dc; join with slip st to first sc: 315 sc.

Rnd 33: Slip st in Front Loop Only of next sc, ch 3, turn; working in Back Loops Only, skip next 2 sts, dc in next 16 sc, (dc, ch 2, dc) in next sc, ★ dc in next 16 sc, skip next 2 sc, dc in next 16 sc, (dc, ch 2, dc) in next sc; repeat from ★ around to last 15 sc, dc in last 15 sc; join with slip st to first dc, finish off: 306 dc and 9 ch-2 sps.

Rnd 34: With **right** side facing, join Pink with dc in any ch-2 sp; dc in same sp, (ch 2, 2 dc in same sp) twice, working in both loops, [skip next 3 dc, (2 dc, ch 2, 2 dc) in next dc] 4 times, skip next 2 dc, [(2 dc, ch 2, 2 dc) in next dc, skip next 3 dc] 4 times, ★ 2 dc in next ch-2 sp, (ch 2, 2 dc in same sp) twice, [skip next 3 dc, (2 dc, ch 2, 2 dc) in next dc] 4 times, skip next 2 dc, [(2 dc, ch 2, 2 dc) in next dc, skip next 3 dc] 4 times; repeat from ★ around; join with slip st to first dc: 90 ch-2 sps.

Rnd 35: Slip st in next dc and in next ch-2 sp, ch 3, do **not** turn; (dc, ch 2, 2 dc) in same sp, (2 dc, ch 2, 2 dc) in next ch-2 sp and in each ch-2 sp around; join with slip st to first dc: 360 dc and 90 ch-2 sps.

Rnd 36: Slip st in next dc and in next ch-2 sp, ch 1, sc in same sp, ch 3, skip next 2 dc, 📹 sc in sp **before** next dc *(Fig. 8, page 31)*, ch 3, ★ sc in next ch-2 sp, ch 3, skip next 2 dc, sc in sp **before** next dc, ch 3; repeat from ★ around; join with slip st to first sc, finish off: 180 ch-3 sps.

Rnd 37: With **right** side facing, 📹 join White with sc in any ch-3 sp *(see Joining With Sc, page 30)*; ch 3, (sc in next ch-3 sp, ch 3) around; join with slip st to first sc, finish off.

Design by Rebecca Leigh.

GENERAL INSTRUCTIONS

ABBREVIATIONS

BPdc	Back Post double crochet(s)
ch(s)	chain(s)
cm	centimeters
dc	double crochet(s)
dtr	double treble crochet(s)
ex Ldc	extended Long double crochet(s)
FP	Front Post
FPdc	Front Post double crochet(s)
hdc	half double crochet(s)
Ldc	Long double crochet(s)
mm	millimeters
Rnd(s)	Round(s)
sc	single crochet(s)
sp(s)	space(s)
st(s)	stitch(es)
tr	treble crochet(s)
YO	yarn over

CROCHET TERMINOLOGY

UNITED STATES		INTERNATIONAL
slip stitch (slip st)	=	single crochet (sc)
single crochet (sc)	=	double crochet (dc)
half double crochet (hdc)	=	half treble crochet (htr)
double crochet (dc)	=	treble crochet(tr)
treble crochet (tr)	=	double treble crochet (dtr)
double treble crochet (dtr)	=	triple treble crochet (ttr)
triple treble crochet (tr tr)	=	quadruple treble crochet (qtr)
skip	=	miss

SYMBOLS & TERMS

★ — work instructions following ★ as many **more** times as indicated in addition to the first time.

† to † — work all instructions from first † to second † **as many** times as specified.

( ) or [ ] — work enclosed instructions **as many** times as specified by the number immediately following **or** work all enclosed instructions in the stitch or space indicated **or** contains explanatory remarks.

colon (:) — the number(s) given after a colon at the end of a row or round denote(s) the number of stitches or spaces you should have on that row or round.

Yarn Weight Symbol & Names	LACE 0	SUPER FINE 1	FINE 2	LIGHT 3	MEDIUM 4	BULKY 5	SUPER BULKY 6
Type of Yarns in Category	Fingering, 10-count crochet thread	Sock, Fingering Baby	Sport, Baby	DK, Light Worsted	Worsted, Afghan, Aran	Chunky, Craft, Rug	Bulky, Roving
Crochet Gauge* Ranges in Single Crochet to 4" (10 cm)	32-42 double crochets**	21-32 sts	16-20 sts	12-17 sts	11-14 sts	8-11 sts	5-9 sts
Advised Hook Size Range	Steel*** 6,7,8 Regular hook B-1	B-1 to E-4	E-4 to 7	7 to I-9	I-9 to K-10.5	K-10.5 to M-13	M-13 and larger

*GUIDELINES ONLY: The chart above reflects the most commonly used gauges and hook sizes for specific yarn categories.

** Lace weight yarns are usually crocheted on larger-size hooks to create lacy openwork patterns. Accordingly, a gauge range is difficult to determine. Always follow the gauge stated in your pattern.

*** Steel crochet hooks are sized differently from regular hooks–the higher the number the smaller the hook, which is the reverse of regular hook sizing.

CROCHET HOOKS

Metric mm	U.S.
2.25	B-1
2.75	C-2
3.25	D-3
3.5	E-4
3.75	F-5
4	G-6
5	H-8
5.5	I-9
6	J-10
6.5	K-10½
8	L-11
9	M/N-13
10	N/P-15
15	P/Q
16	Q
19	S

◼◻◻◻ BEGINNER		Projects for first-time crocheters using basic stitches. Minimal shaping.
◼◼◻◻ EASY		Projects using yarn with basic stitches, repetitive stitch patterns, simple color changes, and simple shaping and finishing.
◼◼◼◻ INTERMEDIATE		Projects using a variety of techniques, such as basic lace patterns or color patterns, mid-level shaping and finishing.
◼◼◼◼ EXPERIENCED		Projects with intricate stitch patterns, techniques and dimension, such as non-repeating patterns, multi-color techniques, fine threads, small hooks, detailed shaping and refined finishing.

GAUGE

Exact gauge is **essential** for proper size. Before beginning your project, make the sample swatch given in the individual instructions in the yarn and hook specified. After completing the swatch, measure it, counting your stitches and rows or rounds carefully. If your swatch is larger or smaller than specified, **make another, changing hook size to get the correct gauge.** Keep trying until you find the size hook that will give you the specified gauge.

JOINING WITH SC

When instructed to join with sc, begin with a slip knot on the hook. Insert the hook in the stitch or space indicated, YO and pull up a loop, YO and draw through both loops on hook.

JOINING WITH DC

When instructed to join with a dc, begin with a slip knot on the hook. YO, holding loop on the hook, insert the hook in the stitch or space indicated, YO and pull up a loop (3 loops on hook), (YO and draw through 2 loops on hook) twice.

BACK OR FRONT LOOP ONLY

Work only in loop(s) indicated by arrow *(Fig. 5)*.

Fig. 5

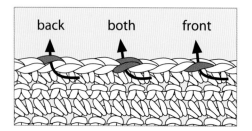

FREE LOOPS OF BEGINNING CHAIN

When instructed to work in free loops of a chain, work in the loop indicated by arrow *(Fig. 6)*.

Fig. 6

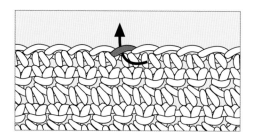

POST STITCH

Work around post of stitch indicated, inserting hook in direction of arrow *(Fig. 7)*.

Fig. 7

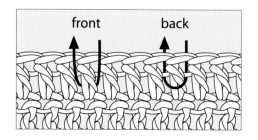

WORKING IN A SPACE BEFORE A STITCH

When instructed to work in space **before** a stitch or in a space **between** stitches, insert hook in space indicated by arrow *(Fig. 8)*.

Fig. 8

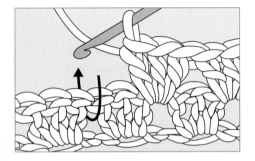

WHIPSTITCH

Place two Motifs, Squares, Panels, or Strips with **wrong** sides together. Sew through both pieces once to secure the beginning of the seam, leaving an ample yarn end to weave in later. Insert the needle from **front** to **back** through **both** loops of each stitch on **both** pieces or through **inside** loops only of each stitch on **both** pieces *(Fig. 9a or 9b)*. Bring the needle around and insert it from **front** to **back** through next loops of both pieces. Continue in this manner across, keeping the sewing yarn fairly loose.

Fig. 9a

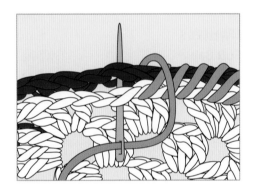

Fig. 9b

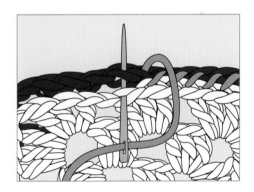

YARN INFORMATION

Each project in this book was made using Light Weight or Medium Weight Yarn. Any brand of the specified weight of yarn may be used. It is best to refer to the yardage/meters when determining how many balls or skeins to purchase. Remember, to arrive at the finished size, it is the GAUGE/TENSION that is important, not the brand of yarn.

For your convenience, listed below are the specific yarns used to create our photography models.

SOFT ZIGZAGS
Red Heart® Soft Baby Steps®
White - #9600 White
Blue - #9800 Baby Blue

TWIRLING PINWHEELS
Red Heart® Soft Baby®
#7001 White

GRANNY'S LOVE
Red Heart® Baby TLC®
White - #5011 White
Blue - #5881 Powder Blue
Yellow - #5322 Powder Yellow
Pink - #5737 Powder Pink
Green - #7624 Lime

LITTLE BOY BLUE
Red Heart® Designer Sport™
#3820 Denim

BABY LOVE
Patons® Astra™
White - #02751 White
Pink - #02752 Baby Pink

CONCENTRIC CIRCLES
Bernat® Softee Baby
White - #02000 White
Lilac - #30185 Soft Lilac
Green - #30221 Soft Fern
Pink - #02001 Pink
Yellow - #02003 Lemon
Blue - #02002 Pale Blue
Mint - #02004 Mint

PRECIOUS IN PINK
Bernat® Softee® Baby
#02001 Pink

RIPPLES OF JOY
Bernat® Satin
MC - #04732 Maitai
Color A - #04005 Snow
Color B - #04423 Flamingo

We have made every effort to ensure that these instructions are accurate and complete. We cannot, however, be responsible for human error, typographical mistakes, or variations in individual work.

Production Team: Writers/Technical Editors - Lois J. Long and Susan Wiles; Editorial Writer - Susan McManus Johnson; Senior Graphic Artist - Lora Puls; Graphic Artists - Becca Snider Tally and Stacy Owens; Photo Stylist - Sondra Daniel; and Photographer - Ken West.

Your opinion matters!

WE WOULD LOVE TO HEAR if our online video instructions and the new format of our publications are helpful to you!

PLEASE SHARE your comments and suggestions at www.facebook.com/Official.LeisureArts